GW00367583

TIBETAN
TING-SHA

TIBETAN
TING-SHA

Sacred sound for
spiritual growth

Robert Beer

CONNECTIONS
BOOK PUBLISHING

A CONNECTIONS EDITION
This edition published in Great Britain in 2004 by
Connections Book Publishing Limited
St Chad's House, 148 King's Cross Road
London WC1X 9DH
www.connections-publishing.com

This edition published in the U.S.A. in 2004 by
Connections Book Publishing Limited.
Distributed in the U.S.A. by Red Wheel/Weiser,
368 Congress Street, Boston, MA 02210.

British Library Cataloguing-in-Publication data available on request.

ISBN 1-85906-153-2

1 3 5 7 9 10 8 6 4 2

Phototypeset in Oneleigh and Zapf Humanist BT 601 using QuarkXPress
on Apple Macintosh
Origination by Bright Arts, Singapore
Printed and bound by Sirivatana Interprint Public Co., Ltd, Thailand

Contents

Introduction

*T*wo Buddhist monks left their hermitage at dawn to return to their teacher's monastery. They had just completed a silent retreat, and walked together across the rugged landscape maintaining their vow of silence. At midday they came upon a swollen river, which a young woman in silk clothes was trying unsuccessfully to cross. Observing her plight the younger monk lifted the woman up and carried her safely across the river, much to the disdain of the elder monk.

Just after sunset they arrived at the monastery, where their vow of silence was broken by their teacher's welcoming enquiries. The elder monk was the first to speak, saying: 'Master, it is forbidden for us monks to touch or even raise our eyes to a woman. Yet earlier today we came across an attractive young woman who was trying to cross a river, and my younger companion actually picked her up in his arms and carried her across.'

The master turned to the younger monk and asked, 'What have you to say in answer to this accusation?'

'I put her down at the riverside,' replied the young monk. 'Why does my elder brother still carry her?'

I first heard this Zen Buddhist story in 1967 on Timothy Leary's album *The Psychedelic Experience*, where the penetrating ring of a Tibetan *ting-sha* punctuated each spoken section. Memory can be both selective and persistent, and from my single hearing of this album I remember only the haunting sound of the ting-sha and the two classical Zen stories that were related on it.

In 1970 I was living in the Tibetan refugee settlement of McLoed Ganj, which is situated above the town of Dharamsala in the foothills of the Indian Himalayas. On one of the Tibetan stalls in this then sleepy little township I came upon a pair of small bronze hand cymbals. When I picked them up and struck them together I immediately recalled my first hearing of them several years earlier, and the Zen tale of non-attachment related above instantly sprang to mind. I asked the Tibetan stallholder what these cymbals were called and used for. She told me they were known as ting-sha and were used in rituals to help both the dead and the tormented spirits. Then I recalled that Timothy Leary's album was based upon his loose interpretation of the Tibetan manual known as the *Tibetan Book of the Dead*. I was struck by the synchronicity of this chance event.

Over the course of the next few years I came across many other pairs of ting-sha on refugee stalls, and was shown sets friends had bought. The beautiful and enduring ring of these cymbals always captivated me, yet the Zen parable of non-attachment prompted me not to possess them, but simply to put them down again on the stall.

During my initial five-year stay in India and Nepal I divided my time between studying Tibetan art in the relative coolness of the Himalayan summers, and Indian classical music in the ancient Hindu city of Varanasi during the winter months. It was through these two disciplines that my understanding of Vajrayana Buddhism and Indian culture began to develop, and I have continued to deepen this understanding over the last thirty years.

This little book is based upon this research. Within the constraints of space I have tried to provide as much information as possible on Tibetan ting-sha and the related use of finger cymbals in other Eastern traditions. The first part of this book tells you about how the cymbals are made and played, and describes the symbolism associated with them. The second part of the book looks at their traditional uses. Finally, there are suggestions for using the cymbals yourself. I hope that the ring of this enchanting instrument may help bring real peace and harmony into your life.

Robert Beer
Oxford, February 2004

The Hand Cymbals

or ting-sha

*T*he mellifluous ring of the small Tibetan hand cymbals known as ting-sha instantly strikes a resonance within the human heart. Their purpose is to summon. They call us to awareness, to mindfully remember who we are, and to recognize our priorities in this often turbulent and changeable world.

The Tibetan term *ting* refers to the ringing sound of metal, to the cadence of a musical note or to the small silver, bronze or bell metal offering bowls placed on a Buddhist altar. The term *sha* means 'hanging' or 'suspended'. The word *ting-sha* may thus be taken to mean either hanging cymbals of bell metal or a sustained musical note.

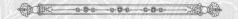

HARMONIC VIBRATION

How to play your ting-sha

Ting-sha are easy to play. They can be picked up and struck immediately. No musical training or tuning ability is needed. Your identical cymbals each measure 64 mm (2½ inches) in diameter and are pitched in approximately the key of E major. The audible duration of their ring is around 12 seconds. Their harmonic frequency creates a diminuendo, or dying away, of oscillating vibrations or sound waves.

There are three principal techniques for striking the ting-sha to create a sustained ring (*see below*). These are all performed in front of the player's heart. The leather thong is held between fingers and thumb just above the centre of each cymbal.

Innovative techniques combining the ring of a ting-sha with the echoing effect of the open larynx or voice box have recently become popular in modern 'new age' spiritual music, particularly in performances featuring 'Tibetan singing bowls'. These techniques are modelled upon the

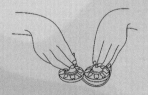

◀ *1. Suspend the ting-sha horizontally, a few inches apart, then draw them together so that their edges strike.*

style of Mongolian overtone chanting, known as *hoomi* singing, in which an ethereal range of high harmonic notes or 'overtones' is simultaneously produced from the low-octave reverberations of the vocal cords. These vocal techniques are relatively easy to accomplish but quite difficult to explain.

For chanting, mantra recitation and dance rhythms, the ting-sha may be repetitively clashed together in the 'face-to-face' manner of conventional hand cymbals. Here their sustained 'open' ring may be replaced by a dampened 'closed' tone by pressing the fingertips onto the upper surfaces of the ting-sha. These methods are used for playing the small brass Indian hand cymbals or *talam*, which are rhythmically employed in dance performances and devotional singing.

As hanging chimes, the ting-sha may be suspended by their leather thong from two hooks and struck with a wooden striker. The paired ting-sha may also be separated to create two individual cymbals, with a striker attached to each end of the divided leather thong. The individual ting-sha was commonly employed in Tibet.

◄ 2. *Suspend one ting-sha horizontally while holding the downward-striking ting-sha vertically in the opposite hand.*

◄ 3. *Hold both ting-sha vertically, at right angles, and strike their edges together with a simultaneous movement of both hands.*

CASTING THE CYMBALS
How your ting-sha are made

Unlike most modern metal products, which are die-cast and machine-milled to a standard industrial precision, these ting-sha have been individually handcrafted by the ancient Tibetan method of sand-casting. The prototype or 'blank' used to make your ting-sha was originally brought out of Tibet in 1959 by a family of refugee bell-casters from eastern Tibet, who resettled in the north Indian town of Dehra Dun in the Himalayan foothills. Since then they have continued their craft of casting ritual bells and ting-sha, passing on their traditional skills from one generation to the next.

Sand-casting techniques differ from the 'lost wax' methods conventionally employed in the casting of bronze statuary. In the lost wax method, the object to be cast is first sculpted in wax and then encased within a wet clay mould. When dry, the mould is heated to melt away the wax and leave a precise clay cavity into which the molten metal is poured. In the sand-casting technique employed for bell casings and ting-sha, an upper and lower mould are fashioned from fine wet sand. This is mixed with an adhesive binder of melted molasses or radish juice. Both sides of the ting-sha 'blanks' are pressed into separate sand moulds, then carefully separated to reveal the precise imprints of the ting-sha's upper and lower surfaces. For expediency, groups of four ting-sha are usually prepared at once, and each is carefully inspected for flaws before they are all gently baked several times over a charcoal fire. The paired moulds are then wire-bound together, and the molten bell metal is poured from a crucible into a small aperture in the centre of the top mould. After several minutes, the sand moulds are broken open and the red-hot ting-sha are left to cool.

European bell metal is traditionally composed of a bronze alloy of copper and tin, to which small amounts of lead and zinc may also be added. But the bell metal used in your ting-sha is composed of a pure bronze alloy of copper and tin, with a white metal component of zinc and nickel. The nickel or 'German silver' used has been specially imported from Germany.

After casting, each individual ting-sha is skilfully tuned by hammering around the thick outer rim to create a per-fectly matching pitch for each pair. They are then mounted onto a simple lathe and polished with an abrasive pad of wet sand on leather. Finally the paired ting-sha are joined together with a leather thong.

THE SYMBOLS ON THE CYMBALS
The design motifs on the ting-sha

The earliest forms of Tibetan ting-sha were unadorned and modelled upon the Indian *talam (see page 33)*. The embellished forms probably first appeared in the late nineteenth century, with the motifs of the 'Eight Auspicious Symbols' of Buddhism embossed upon their upper surfaces. Your ting-sha are based upon this early prototype. With the development of the Oriental tourist market over the last few decades, it has now become common practice to introduce new decorative designs on ting-sha. These include paired dragons, scrolling lotus designs, conch shells, and the six-syllable mantra of Avalokiteshvara: *Om Mani Padme Hum*.

Your paired ting-sha are embossed on their convex upper surfaces with the Eight Auspicious Symbols and a lotus design of eight petals on their central bosses. Their concave undersides are engraved with the three sacred Tibetan syllables: *Om A Hum (see also page 25)*.

Om   *A*   *Hum*

THE EIGHT AUSPICIOUS SYMBOLS

The Eight Auspicious Symbols are of ancient Indian origin. They actually predate the advent of Buddhism, which developed during the lifetime of the historical Buddha, Shakyamuni (*circa* 566–486 BCE). Eight heavenly goddesses were reputed to have presented these eight propitious objects to the great sky god Indra, who was regarded as the 'king of the gods' in ancient Indian Vedic mythology. These eight symbols were later grouped into an assembly of offerings that were presented before an earthly Indian king at his investiture. Variations of these royal symbols appeared in both the early Hindu and Jain traditions.

The Buddhists similarly adopted a group of Eight Auspicious Symbols as a representation of the supreme sovereignty of the Buddha's teachings. These eight symbolic objects are: (1) a white parasol; (2) a golden treasure vase; (3) a pair of golden fishes; (4) a lotus; (5) a victory banner; (6) a white conch shell that spirals towards the right; (7) an endless knot or 'lucky diagram'; (8) a golden wheel.

In the Buddhist tradition these Eight Auspicious Symbols represent the offerings presented to Shakyamuni Buddha upon his attainment of enlightenment. They symbolize the 'Eightfold Noble Path' that leads to the cessation of suffering and enlightenment. This path consists of cultivating: (1)

1

2

3

4

5

6

7

8

correct view or understanding; (2) correct thought or analysis; (3) correct speech; (4) correct action; (5) correct livelihood; (6) correct effort; (7) correct mindfulness; (8) correct concentration or meditative stability.

In Chinese Buddhism these eight symbols represent the eight vital organs of the Buddha's body: (1) the parasol represents his spleen; (2) the treasure vase his stomach; (3) the two golden fishes his kidneys; (4) the lotus his liver; (5) the victory banner his lungs; (6) the conch shell his gall bladder; (7) the endless knot his intestines; and (8) the golden wheel his heart. A similar Tibetan tradition identifies these eight symbols as forming the physical body of the Buddha, with: (1) the parasol representing his head; (2) the treasure vase his neck; (3) the golden fishes his eyes; (4) the lotus his tongue; (5) the victory banner his body; (6) the conch his speech; (7) the endless knot his mind; and (8) the golden wheel his limbs.

In Sanskrit (Skt), these symbols are known as the *ashta-mangala*, and in Tibetan (Tib.) as the *Tashi-targey*. In the Indian Buddhist tradition they were later deified into a group of eight offering goddesses, known as the Astamangala Devi, each of whom carried one of the auspicious symbols as an attribute. These Eight Auspicious Symbols are embossed around each of your ting-sha in a clockwise sequence, beginning with the parasol.

The Parasol
(Skt *chatra, atapatra*; Tib. *gdugs*)

The parasol is an Indian symbol of royalty and protection. Its shadow protects from the blazing heat of the sun. The coolness of its shade symbolizes protection from the painful heat of suffering, obstacles, illnesses and harmful forces. As the parasol is held above the head, it naturally symbolizes honour and respect; the image of a parasol above an empty throne was originally used as a representation of the Buddha. A retinue of thirteen parasol bearers traditionally accompanied an Indian king, and this symbolism was incorporated into the design of the Buddha's *stupa* or 'reliquary monument' as an ascending pinnacle of thirteen 'umbrella wheels'.

An elaborate parasol is often depicted above the head of a Buddha or Bodhisattva. This jewelled parasol was symbolically offered to the Buddha by the king of the serpent-spirits or *nagas*. Traditionally depicted with a long sandalwood handle, this auspicious parasol is embellished at its top with a radiating wish-granting gem. Its domed frame is covered with white silk, and from the circular golden rim of this frame hangs a frieze of multicoloured silk pendants, valances and billowing ribbons. The parasol's white dome represents wisdom, and its hanging valances the various methods of compassion or 'skilful means'.

2

The Treasure Vase
(Skt *nidhana-kumbha*; Tib. *gter-gyi bum-pa*)

The golden treasure vase, or 'vase of inexhaustible wealth', was presented to the Buddha by the goddess of the earth, Sthavara, after he had called upon her in the hour of his enlightenment to bear witness to his countless acts of sacrifice. The treasure vase is predominantly a symbol of certain wealth deities, where it often appears filled with jewels beneath their feet. The treasure vase is modelled on the traditional Indian water pot, known as a *kalasha* or *kumbha*, with a flat base, round body, narrow neck and fluted rim. In Vedic mythology this pot is also identified with the vase of 'immortal nectar' (Skt *amrita*) possessed by the gods. A single wish-granting gem or a group of three gems usually seals the treasure vase's upper rim as a symbol of the 'Three Jewels' of the Buddha, his teachings (Skt *dharma*) and his monastic community (Skt *sangha*).

Sealed Tibetan treasure vases are often placed or buried at sacred locations – such as pilgrimage sites, mountain passes, springs, rivers and lakes – where they function both to spread abundance and to appease the indigenous spirits who abide in these places. The golden treasure vase essentially symbolizes the inexhaustible wealth of the Buddha's teachings.

The Pair of Golden Fishes
(Skt *suvarnamatsya*; Tib. *gser-nya*)

The auspicious symbol of a pair of golden fishes was probably presented to the Buddha as an embroidery design of gold thread upon a length of folded silk. The motif of a pair of fishes is common to the Hindu, Jain and Buddhist traditions; originally it appeared as an ancient symbol of the two great sacred rivers of India, the Ganges and Yamuna. Symbolically, these two rivers represent the two main subsidiary channels or 'psychic nerves' (Skt *nadi*) of the 'subtle energy body', which originate in the nostrils and carry the alternating rhythms of breath or vital energy (Skt *prana*).

In Buddhism, the paired golden fishes represent happiness and spontaneity, as they have complete freedom of movement in the water. They symbolize fertility and abundance, as they multiply very rapidly. As they mingle and touch readily, they also represent freedom from the constraints of caste and status. In China, a pair of fishes symbolizes conjugal unity and fidelity, with a brace of fishes being traditionally given as a wedding present. As fish were so plentiful in China, the Chinese word *yu*, meaning both 'fish' and 'great wealth', became synonymous with material prosperity. In the Chinese tradition of feng shui, the keeping of goldfish is similarly believed to attract wealth.

3

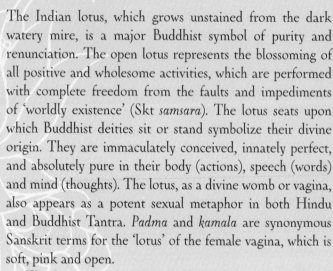

The Lotus
(Skt *padma, kamala*; Tib. *pad-ma, chu-skyes*)

The Indian lotus, which grows unstained from the dark watery mire, is a major Buddhist symbol of purity and renunciation. The open lotus represents the blossoming of all positive and wholesome activities, which are performed with complete freedom from the faults and impediments of 'worldly existence' (Skt *samsara*). The lotus seats upon which Buddhist deities sit or stand symbolize their divine origin. They are immaculately conceived, innately perfect, and absolutely pure in their body (actions), speech (words) and mind (thoughts). The lotus, as a divine womb or vagina, also appears as a potent sexual metaphor in both Hindu and Buddhist Tantra. *Padma* and *kamala* are synonymous Sanskrit terms for the 'lotus' of the female vagina, which is soft, pink and open.

The lotus may be described as having eight, sixteen, thirty-two, sixty-four, a hundred or a thousand petals. Symbolically, these numbers relate to the lotus-circles of mandala designs and to the 'channel wheels' (Skt *nadi-chakra*) of the body's refined 'subtle energy plexuses' or chakras. A lotus with eight petals essentially represents the heart centre or chakra as the 'seat of the mind'. This eight-petal lotus of the heart is similarly represented upon the central bosses of your ting-sha.

The Victory Banner
(Skt *dhvaja*; Tib. *rgyal-mtshan*)

The victory banner was originally a military standard of ancient Indian warfare. These ensigns distinguished the chariots of India's epic heroes, and were frequently adorned with ferocious animal heads, such as the tiger and crocodile. The crocodile-headed banner was an emblem of Kamadeva, the Vedic god of desire. As the 'tempter' (Skt *mara*), Kamadeva was identified by the early Buddhists as the destructive god Mara, who attempted to obstruct the Buddha's enlightenment by assailing him with the four divisions of his army. As a symbol of the Buddha's victory over these 'four maras', four directional victory banners were later erected around the Buddha's reliquary monument or *stupa*. The roofs of Tibetan monasteries are similarly ornamented with four victory banners as a symbol of the Buddha's triumph over all obstructive forces.

A small white parasol and a wish-granting gem surmount the victory banner. The rim of this parasol is ornamented with a golden crest-bar, the edges of which turn upwards to form scrolling 'crocodile-tail' embellishments. The cylindrical upper part of the victory banner is composed of many layers of hanging silk valances, while its lower part consists of pleated and billowing silk. Jewel chains and silk ribbons adorn the banner, and it often has an upper frieze of tiger skin, symbolizing the Buddha's triumph over all aggression.

5

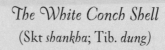

The White Conch Shell
(Skt *shankha*; Tib. *dung*)

6

The white conch shell, which spirals in a clockwise direction, was originally an ancient Indian attribute of the heroic gods, whose mighty conch shell horns proclaimed their valour and victory in warfare. Although rare in nature, the right-spiralling conch represents the true or 'right-hand path' of established religious doctrine, as opposed to the more common left-spiralling conch, which symbolizes the shadowy 'left-hand path' of shamanism and goddess worship. The tip of the conch shell is sawn off to form a mouthpiece, and its wind passage that spirals outward in a clockwise direction symbolizes the Buddha's 'right-hand' proclamation of the *dharma* or religious law. The auspicious blast of the conch shell horn is still commonly heard in India's temples, where it serves to summon the gods and to banish all evil spirits, harmful creatures and natural disasters.

The conch is primarily an attribute of Vishnu, the great Vedic 'right-hand god' of preservation. In the Hindu tradition, Shakyamuni Buddha is regarded as the ninth of Vishnu's ten incarnations or *avatars*, and in Buddhist art the Vedic god Indra is often portrayed offering Vishnu's mighty conch to the Buddha. The white conch symbolizes the supremacy of the Buddha's teachings, which he triumphantly proclaims throughout space and time.

The Glorious Endless Knot
(Skt *shrivatsa, granthi*; Tib. *dpal-be'u*)

The glorious eternal knot is usually depicted as an endlessly woven knot of gold. Its innovative forms are commonly found in many ancient traditions, such as in Celtic and Islamic design. In Sanskrit, this knot is known as the *shrivatsa*, meaning 'beloved of Shri', referring to the prosperity goddess Lakshmi, consort of Vishnu. The shrivatsa was originally an auspicious mark or hair-curl that adorned Vishnu's breast as a symbol of his love and devotion. In China, the endless knot is known as the 'lucky diagram', and symbolizes longevity, continuity, love and harmony.

As a symbol of continuity and harmony, the shrivatsa is often identified with another ancient symbol of eternal stability, the swastika. In ancient Taoist China, this was a symbol of the 'ten thousand things under heaven'. The Sanskrit word *svastika* derives from the root *svasti*, meaning good fortune, success or prosperity. The Buddha, as the ninth of Vishnu's ten incarnations, is often shown with a swastika adorning his breast as a symbol of his auspicious mind. In Buddhism this knot represents the continuity and perfect integration of the wisdom and compassion of the Buddha's enlightened mind.

7

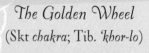

The Golden Wheel
(Skt *chakra*; Tib. *'khor-lo*)

An early Indian solar symbol, the wheel first appeared on clay seals from the ancient Indus valley civilization (*circa* 2500 BCE). As a rimless weapon of six or eight sharp blades, the wheel or *chakra* was originally a discus wielded by Vishnu, the *mahapurusha* or 'great man' born with the divine insignia of a thousand-spoke wheel on his palms and soles. The Buddha was likewise blessed with these divine marks, and as the destined 'wheel-turning monarch' or *chakravartin* he set in motion the 'wheel of transformation' (Skt *dharmachakra*) of his spiritual teachings.

The three main early discourses of the Buddha are known as his first, second and third 'turnings of the wheel of *dharma*'. The emblem of an eight-spoke golden wheel flanked by two deer became an enduring symbol of his first discourse in the Deer Park at Sarnath, near Varanasi. This wheel is known as a *dharmachakra*. Its three components of hub, spokes and rim symbolize the Buddha's three collective teachings upon ethics, wisdom and meditation. Its eight spokes represent the Buddha's 'Eightfold Noble Path' that leads to the cessation of suffering, with the sharpness of these spokes symbolizing the discriminating awareness that cuts through ignorance.

THE THREE SYLLABLES
Enlightened body, speech and mind

Om

The concave undersides of your ting-sha are polished to resemble a mirror. They are inscribed in each of the four cardinal directions with the three sacred Tibetan syllables *Om A Hum*, and a fourth character that functions as a full stop. The three syllables may also be transliterated and pronounced in English as '*Om Ah Hung*'.

A

The three syllables are engraved in an anticlockwise sequence. They represent the three aspects of enlightened body (Om), speech (A) and mind (Hum). These correspond to the spiritual concept of purity in deed (body), word (speech) and thought (mind). Virtually all Buddhist deity practices recite these three important mantra syllables. Traditionally, they are visualized in colour at their respective energy centres of the crown of the head (white Om), the throat (red A) and the heart (blue Hum). They are respectively inscribed at these points on the back surface of a deity painting or *thangka*, where they serve to consecrate or 'empower' the main central figure.

Hum

The syllables also symbolize the transmutation of the 'three poisons' of ignorance (white Om), desire (red A) and aggression (blue Hum) into the three enlightened qualities of wisdom, compassion and power. In addition, they represent the three 'divine bodies of a Buddha': the physical 'form or emanation body' (white Om), the visionary 'enjoyment body' (red A) and the pure empty 'truth or *dharma* body' (blue Hum). These divine bodies correspond to the three 'intermediary states' of the death experience (*see page 28*), and to the three 'everyday states' of waking, dream and deep sleep.

The fourth character, represented by two small circles separated by a short horizontal line, is known in Tibetan as a *ter-shay*. This full-stop symbol is frequently found at the end of a mantra, and indicates that the mantra was revealed through a *terma* or 'hidden treasure' text. These concealed 'treasure texts' are mainly believed to have been hidden during the eighth century by the great Indian Tantric master, Padmasambhava, who is essentially credited with bringing Buddhism to Tibet. Throughout the centuries these hidden treasures have been rediscovered by a succession of enlightened 'treasure finders' or *tertons*, whose tasks have been to reveal these esoteric teachings into the light of their own time. Perhaps the most famous of these revealed treasure texts is the *Bardo Thodol*, commonly known as the *Tibetan Book of the Dead*, which was discovered in a mountain face during the fourteenth century by a great Tibetan treasure finder named Karma Lingpa.

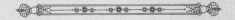

Traditional Uses

Within the many and varied Tibetan Buddhist rituals and meditation practices, the ting-sha are actually employed in only a few specific rituals. Their principal use is to summon or call forth, with their high-pitched reverberation penetrating into ethereal realms that extend beyond the senses of mortal man. The main rituals in which the ting-sha are struck are in guidance prayers and food offerings for the dead; in burned food and water offerings for the 'hungry ghosts' or tormented spirits; in burned food offerings to the 'four classes of guests'.

These rituals are often performed as solitary practices by many Tibetan monks, some of whom have chosen to perform them every day of their lives, or as a cycle of a hundred thousand offerings. Such dedicated practitioners would never sound their ting-sha without also presenting an offering of burned food or water for the 'honoured guests' or wandering spirits.

(1) Samantabhadra (truth body)

(2) Amitayus (example of enjoyment body)

(3) Garab Dorje (example of emanation body)

RITUALS OF GUIDANCE FOR THE DEAD

Prayers for the dead are traditionally recited for forty-nine days after a person's death. Symbolically, this period represents the time during which the consciousness of the deceased undergoes the transition from its former to its future life. Three distinct intervals or 'intermediary states' (Tib. *bardo*) are recognized during this period, which correspond symbolically to the 'three divine bodies' of a Buddha.

The first is the bardo of the death experience itself, when the dissolution of the gross physical life force leads to the direct experience of the subtle 'clear light' of the innate mind (truth body) (1). The second is the bardo of 'actual reality', when the deceased's consciousness experiences the visionary manifestation of the 'peaceful and wrathful deities' (enjoyment body) (2). The third is the bardo of 'seeking rebirth', when the disembodied consciousness takes on another physical form (emanation body) (3).

These three intermediary states are symbolically described in the *Bardo Thodol*. Tibetan lamas and monks are traditionally employed to recite the daily prayers of guidance during this period, the ring of the ting-sha serving to summon the deceased's consciousness. Burned food and water are offered to the deceased, as a wandering spirit can only imbibe scents.

THE HUNGRY GHOSTS OR *PRETAS*

Depending upon one's own accumulation of previous karma, rebirth can occur in one of the 'six realms' of cyclic existence or *samsara*. Three of these realms are classed as fortunate or 'higher realms' – the gods, demi-gods and human realms – and three are unfortunate or 'lower realms' – the animals, hungry ghosts and hell realms.

The main cause of rebirth into the *preta* or hungry ghost realm is extreme avarice and miserliness. The denizens of this miserable realm are believed to experience insatiable hunger and thirst. Many of these hungry ghosts are described as having enormous stomachs, frail limbs, reed-like necks with knots in them, and pinhole mouths. They collectively inhabit barren landscapes of extreme heat and cold, where they are perpetually afflicted by hallucinations in their endless search for food and water. Some breathe and excrete fire, while others are covered in dry skin, bristling hair or festering sores. Even if they manage to find a trace of food or water, they are unable to swallow even a morsel, as like a mirage it evaporates or transforms into putrid filth before their famished eyes.

Other forms of pretas are classified as 'tormented spirits'. They travel through space seeking to transfer their afflictions of insanity, disease and disturbance through possessing the life force of another being.

The Burned Food or sur Ritual for the Hungry Ghosts

The enduring misery of these hungry ghosts is excruciating. To temporarily alleviate their insatiable hunger and thirst, rituals offering burned food and poured water are regularly performed. The burned food offering is known as the *sur* ritual, and is performed by sounding the ting-sha while burning a specific food on an ember of glowing charcoal. The ghost or spirit as a 'scent-eater' is attracted by the summons of the ting-sha, and gains some immediate satisfaction by imbibing the scent-laden smoke of the burning food. For a moment in time the hungry ghost is released from its obsessive craving and able to hear the specific mantra and prayer of the chanting monk, who seeks to liberate it from bondage. Such a recited prayer is:

> *Abandon all evil actions.*
> *Practise only virtue.*
> *Learn to master your own mind.*
> *This is the teaching of the Buddha.*

The sur offering is of two kinds: the 'white offering' and the 'red offering'. The white consists of small balls of barley flour mixed with the 'three white substances' of milk, curd and ghee (clarified butter), and the 'three sweet substances' of sugar, molasses and honey. The red consists of meat.

THE WATER *TORMA* AND *SUR* OFFERING FOR THE FOUR CLASSES OF GUESTS

The water offering is known as a water *torma* and is made with a mixture of water, milk and grains. The ritual is performed with a ting-sha, ritual prayer and a water-offering set, which consists of a small metal bowl mounted upon a tripod, the feet of which rest in a larger metal bowl. The liquid is poured from a spouted water-pot into the smaller upper bowl until it spills over to fill the larger lower bowl. The liquid is then poured back into the water-pot, the ting-sha struck again, and the prayer repeated as the water is again poured into the upper bowl.

The sur offering for the 'four classes of guests' is performed with a variety of different burned foods for the various 'guests'. The first class are the 'guests to be venerated', consisting of the Buddhas, Bodhisattvas and lineage teachers. The second class are the 'guests with good qualities', consisting of the protective deities. The third class are the 'guests to whom one must be compassionate', consisting of beings within the six realms of cyclic existence. The fourth class are the 'guests to whom you have a karmic debt or obligation', consisting of those beings that seek revenge and retribution for all the harm you have bestowed on them in previous lives.

DIVINE MUSICIANS AND OFFERING GODDESSES

Certain categories of celestial spirits serve as the musicians and physicians of the gods. In Sanskrit they are known as *gandharvas* (Tib. *dri-za*) or 'scent-eaters'. The gandharvas dwell in beautiful dream-like cities that ascend above the clouds, where they consume the refined fragrances of food and incense, and imbibe mellifluous music and lyrical verse. Their voluptuous, nymph-like consorts are known as *apsaras*, who are similarly skilled in the arts of music, dance and erotic love. Musical prodigies, such as Mozart or Beethoven, may be viewed in both the Hindu and Buddhist traditions as gandharvas that have taken rebirth in a human form.

As an attribute, the ting-sha may be depicted in the hands of an apsara or gandharva. They may also appear in the hands of the Buddhist goddess of sound, Shabda, and either of the two offering goddesses of dance, Lasya and Nritya. As a symbol of harmonious sound, a pair of ting-sha is often depicted in a golden bowl, along with a mirror (sight), a conch shell of perfume (smell), fruit (taste) and a silk cloth (touch), to represent the 'five sensory offerings'. Ting-sha may also appear as an eighth auxiliary offering of sound to the 'seven offering bowls' of a Buddhist altar.

DEVOTIONAL SINGING AND SACRED DANCE

In India, small brass 'finger cymbals' known as *tala* or *talam* are traditionally used to accompany the singing of Hindu devotional songs and prayers. The Indian talam are very similar in appearance and size to the Tibetan ting-sha, but are thinner and lighter, unadorned with symbols, and are strung separately on two short lengths of knotted rope. The talam are played by clashing the two cymbals gently together with an alternating up and down movement to create the rhythmic metre (Skt *tala*) for the syllables of the song or mantra being recited.

Hindu devotional songs are commonly known as *kirtans* or *bhajans*, and usually consist of praises or repetitions of the names and qualities of the various Hindu deities. The most well-known Hindu chant is probably the 'Hari Krishna' mantra, which is frequently performed on the streets of many Western cities by devotees of the Krishna Consciousness Movement. There are literally thousands of such devotional chants within the various sects and traditions of Hinduism, many of which take the form of a 'rosary of the 108 sacred names' of a particular deity. The lead singer of a bhajan group usually chants the first line of a devotional song to the rhythmic accompaniment of the finger cymbals, while the

other members of the group collectively repeat the refrain or second line. A double-sided hand drum or a pair of tabla drums may also be used to provide the rhythm in bhajan performances, while the accompanying melody is usually played on a harmonium.

Talam are also used in classical Indian dance perform-ances, with the dance master or choreographer sitting to one side of the stage and reciting the various rhythmic dance patterns to the tempo of the cymbals. A similar pair of fin-ger cymbals, known as *ta*, is used in the Buddhist 'spiritual dance' (Skt *charya-nritya*) traditions of Nepal, which date back over a thousand years and are performed as invoca-tions to specific Tantric deities. Colourful silk costumes, with bone and jewel ornaments, and headdresses or masks, are traditionally worn in these sacred dances. Along with specific movements, postures and gestures, they enable the dancer to transform themself meditatively into the form of that particular deity. The Sanskrit verses that accompany these dances are based upon the melodic structures of early Indian ragas, and are sung by the *vajracharya* or 'Tantric priest' to the ring of his cymbals. Similar brass finger cym-bals are found throughout Asia, such as the Chinese *po*, the Burmese *si* and the Thai *ching*.

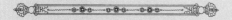

Using Your Ting-sha

*Y*ou can use the ting-sha for your own spiritual purposes, *whatever your tradition or religion. What is important is the knowledge that real spiritual transformation is taking place in your daily life. The Tibetans are a fun-loving people who have encountered a wide spectrum of metaphysical concepts during their years of exile. The following pages give just a few suggestions for using your ting-sha, but as the Sufi mystical poet Rumi so eloquently states: 'There are a hundred ways to kneel and kiss the ground'.*

TINTINNABULATION
Poetry, song and music

In his poem *The Bells*, Edgar Allan Poe skilfully creates four lyrical sentiments from the ringing sound of bells – silver sleigh bells of merriment, golden wedding bells of happiness, brazen alarm bells of fear, and the solemn iron bells of death. In ancient India, nine different sentiments were employed in dance, drama and music to convey the entire range of human emotive expression. These nine sentiments (Skt *navarasa*) are erotic, heroic, repulsive, playful, wrathful, awe-inspiring, compassionate, dignified and peaceful.

The gamut of spiritual sentiment perhaps achieves its finest expression in the *Mathnawi* of Jelaluddin Rumi (1207–73), now the most widely read poet in the Western world. The six volumes of the *Mathnawi* comprise a total of 25,700 verses, each written in a metre of twenty-two syllables, which lends itself perfectly to the acoustic refrain of the ting-sha. Many succinct verse extracts and quatrains of Rumi's work have now been translated into English, as have those of other great Sufi and Hindu poets, such as Hafiz, Ibn 'Arabi, Kabir, Lalla and the Bauls of Bengal. The ting-sha also lend themselves very well to the poetic imagery of Japanese *haiku* verses, which are composed in a metre of seventeen syllables.

Rhythmic chanting in a group situation creates an ecstatic feeling of oneness or 'divine union' among the participants. These techniques may be applied in a variety of spiritual contexts, such as in the singing of prayers, mantras and devotional songs. A simple melodic refrain and rhythmic structure make the lyrics of a song or chant easy to remember, and many religious traditions utilize these methods to consign liturgical texts to memory. The ting-sha may be used for all such vocal rituals, either by striking a sound between verses or as a gentle rhythmic series of 'face-to-face' clashes. In Hindu devotional singing, the rhythm of the hand cymbals is usually complemented melodically with a harmonium, but a guitar or keyboard can be equally effective.

In experimental 'new age' music, the ting-sha can be made to harmonize with a variety of other percussive instruments – such as gongs, drums and xylophones – and drone instruments, such as the didgeridoo and tamboura. One popular modern instrument is the so-called Tibetan singing bowl, which produces a continuous ringing drone when a wooden striker is rubbed around its rim. These bronze bowls were never actually employed in Tibet as ritual instruments, but are now widely produced for the tourist markets of India and Nepal.

*(1) water for drinking
and mouth-rinsing*

*(2) water for washing
the feet*

*(3) flowers to adorn
the hair*

*(4) incense for a
pleasing scent*

OFFERING RITUALS

*When you give, a thousand gifts are given unto you.
When you give with unconditional love,
And with no thought of what you may receive in turn,
What comes back is truly amazing.*

Rituals of offering are common to most spiritual traditions. These often take the form of a sacrificial festival where the 'first fruits' of one's labours are presented in gratitude to the Creative Principal. An altar or high place serves as the conventional receptacle for offerings. You can easily erect a simple shrine upon a shelf or desktop in your own home. Icons, deity statues or photographs of your spiritual mentors can occupy the central place on the shrine, along with bowls containing fresh water, food offerings and flowers, an incense burner, a lamp or candle and your ting-sha (the traditional order of Tibetan offerings is illustrated here, to the left and right). The food offering can consist of sweets, cakes, biscuits, fruits or grains.

Seated before your altar with its freshly prepared offerings, imagine that you are presenting all these auspicious substances to all beings with complete equanimity. As you sound your ting-sha, imagine that your offerings are multiplied a thousand-fold and are received with both gratitude and joy.

At the end of a Buddhist offering ritual, the contents of the water and food bowls are traditionally cast outside for the benefit of any wandering spirits or hungry animals. Birds are often the main recipients of these offerings, and in Indian astrology it is considered auspicious to feed crows and other black birds on Saturdays as a protection against the malevolent influences of the planet Saturn.

Ritual offerings for the 'hungry ghosts' (*see page 29*) should not be performed without instructions from a qualified teacher. At a barbecue, however, you may safely put some pieces of grilled meat in a corner of the garden for the *pretas*. Similarly, rituals of guidance for the dead should not be attempted without adequate training, as the spirit of a deceased person should be allowed to pass unhindered into its next incarnation. In some cases, however, when things have been left unsaid or situations left unresolved, there may be an overwhelming need to communicate with the deceased.

In this situation it is best to unburden your heart only once, clearly revealing your deepest feelings. Love and forgiveness are the greatest gifts you can offer anyone, and you can summon and release the spirit of your loved one with the ring of your ting-sha. It is also beneficial to perform a simple *sur* ritual for forty-nine days after a death (*see page 28*), dedicating the merit of the ritual for an auspicious rebirth of the deceased.

(5) *lamp for the light of wisdom*

(6) *scented water for face-washing*

(7) *torma or food offering*

(8) *ting-sha for musical delight*

The sur Offering Ritual

One simple *sur* ritual involves the visualization of four-armed Avalokiteshvara, the Bodhisattva of compassion. As Tibet's patron deity, he emanates in the successive incarnations of the Dalai Lama. Avalokiteshvara, in his four-armed form, is white in colour and holds a lotus, crys-tal rosary and a wish-granting gem before his heart. His four arms symbolize the 'four immeasurables' of love, compassion, sympathetic joy and equanimity.

To perform the sur offering ritual of 'nourishment through scent for the four classes of guests' (*see page 31*), begin by reciting the prayer of refuge and *bodhichitta* three times:

Until I am enlightened I take refuge
In the Buddha, the dharma and the sublime assembly (sangha).
By the merit that I accumulate from practising the 'six perfections'
May I attain the state of Buddhahood in order to benefit all beings.

The next step is to imagine yourself in the form of four-armed Avalokiteshvara, who purifies the burned food and water offerings by reciting the three syllables of *Ram* (fire), *Yam* (wind) and *Kham* (water), and consecrates the offerings with the three sacred syllables *Om A Hum*. Then recite the prayer to the four classes of guests:

> *These sur offerings are clouds of sense pleasure that extend throughout space.*
> *They are offered to the enlightened deities, the protective deities,*
> *And are compassionately given to all beings, and to all those that hinder us.*
> *May they be delighted and satisfied.*
> *May we perfect skilful means and wisdom, purify all obscurations,*
> *And enjoy the attainments of happiness and enlightenment.*

As you burn the sur offering and strike the ting-sha, recite the six-syllable mantra of Avalokiteshvara: *Om Mani Padme Hum.* Each syllable corresponds to one of the six realms of existence. The sur should consist of flour mixed with a little of the 'three whites' of milk, yogurt and butter, and the 'three sweets' of sugar, molasses and honey. A pinch of this flour can be sprinkled upon a small burning charcoal block, an ember, a hotplate or griddle, and with each sprinkling the prayer and mantra are recited and the ting-sha struck. Traditionally, a cycle of 108 consecutive sur offerings is made, and at the end of the ritual one dedicates the merit of this practice with the prayer:

> *This virtuous accumulation we have offered so that all obstacles are removed,*
> *And at the time of our death all suffering may be eased.*
> *May we swiftly take rebirth in the pure land of Great Bliss,*
> *And quickly attain enlightenment for the benefit of all beings.*

OUTER PURIFICATION
Space-cleansing rituals

'Space cleansing' – or psychic purification of one's environment – is probably the easiest spiritual exercise to perform with the ting-sha. This practice may be done on a regular basis, such as in preparing a sacred and stress-free space for a yoga or meditation session. You might use it for a more specific purpose, such as to psychically cleanse a new home or room of its accumulated impressions; in feng shui practices; or in the marking of new beginnings, such as a New Year's or Midsummer's Eve.

Open the windows of your room or home with the resolution that you are going to banish all negative emotional and psychic impressions from your environment. Sound the ting-sha in each corner of each room, and imagine that their penetrating sound is driving away all these dark influences through the windows. Candles and incense may also be employed in this cleansing ritual, with the gentle circling of a candle flame representing the illumination of wisdom, and the wafting of incense smoke the exorcism of all negative energies. Frankincense and juniper are often traditionally employed for psychic purification; these aromatic substances may be burned either in their raw form on a charcoal block, or as essential oils in a ceramic burner.

INNER PURIFICATION
Samatha *or 'tranquil abiding' meditation*

Many meditation practices require you to focus mentally upon an 'object'. This can be the visualized form of a deity, a mantra, an analytical thought, an esoteric symbol or a yogic energy centre. But the mind's nature is to wander and become distracted, and for the beginner this mental object often proves elusive. For this reason the basic Buddhist meditation practice of *samatha* or 'tranquil abiding' usually takes the breath as the object of concentration, as the process of breathing continues throughout each moment of our existence.

We begin by observing the process of breathing itself, of noticing how the lungs and upper body expand with each inhalation and contract with each exhalation, with a moment of stillness before each new breath. Become aware of the sensations that arise as you breathe, of the air passing into your nostrils, down your throat and into your lungs, and its return passage. Then begin to observe the more subtle sensations as the breath passes over the area between your upper lip and nostrils. When you recognize mental distraction, recall your concentration with a strike of your ting-sha and start again. In time, and with regular practice, you should find that your mind becomes more focused and tranquil.

VIPASSANA OR 'INSIGHT' MEDITATION

Through observing the breath and its sensations (*see 'Inner Purification', page 43*), you will begin to notice that any disturbance in your mind causes a corresponding change in your breathing pattern. If mental agitation, anger, fear or passion arise, you will notice that your breathing becomes stronger and faster. If you look deeper you will also observe that a simultaneous physiological reaction is occurring within your body, creating an unpleasant mental or emotional sensation like a tense knot. Through directly observing and mindfully facing these knots, however, we discover they can dissolve and unravel very quickly.

Once we learn to recognize the internal source of these negativities, which are heralded by a change in both respiration and sensation, then we begin to break the patterns of projecting our frustrations to the external world. Instead of casting blame on others for our problems – and harming them through aggressive actions, harsh words and malevolent thoughts – we begin to purify our body, speech and mind, creating harmony and tranquillity both within ourselves and in our relationships with others. This technique of 'insight meditation' was taught in the 'Four Noble Truths' of the Buddha – the truths of suffering, its origin, its cessation, and the truth of the path leading to its cessation.

PRACTISING LOVING KINDNESS

The foundations of the Buddhist path are built upon the four 'divine abodes' of compassion, love, sympathetic joy and equanimity. These are the 'four immeasurable wishes' that all beings may be free from suffering, enjoy happiness, abide in bliss, and relinquish both attachment and aversion. When you become aware that strangers are friends whom you haven't yet met, and that your perceived enemies are really your teachers in disguise, then you have already embarked upon this spiritual path.

Through the practice of mindfulness and analytical insight, or self-purification through self-observation, we begin to truly know ourselves and to recognize the pure nature of our innate mind. The innate mind is like an immaculately polished mirror, which reflects everything unconditionally and without distortion or blemish. A pure mind is always full of love, compassion, joy and equanimity for the welfare of others.

At the end of every meditation session it is customary to dedicate the merit of one's spiritual practice and insight for the benefit of others. This dedication can be beautifully expressed through the striking of the ting-sha in front of your heart. Each ring of the cymbals acts as a vehicle for the radiation of the 'immeasurable harmony' of your love, compassion, joy and equanimity towards all beings.

Glossary

Bodhichitta (Skt): The altruistic 'mind of enlightenment' that aspires to attain Buddhahood for the sake of all beings.

Bodhisattva (Skt): An 'enlightened hero' on the path to Buddhahood. The divine forms in which manifest many of the peaceful male and female deities of Buddhism.

Dharma (Skt): The teachings of the Buddha, the second of the 'Three Jewels'.

Feng shui (Chinese): Literally 'wind and water'. The ancient Chinese system of geomancy, now widely applied in building design and location.

Jain (Skt): An Indian religious tradition that developed at the same time as Buddhism and has ideological similarities. Its founder was Mahavira, the 'conqueror' (Skt *jina*).

Protective deities (Skt *dharmapala*): The protectors of the Buddhist teachings, usually depicted as the wrathful manifestations of enlightened beings.

Sangha (Skt): The monastic community or practitioners of the Buddha's teachings, the third of the 'Three Jewels'.

Six Perfections (Skt *paramita*): The transcendental practices of generosity, discipline, patience, effort, concentration and wisdom. The first five perfections form the 'accumulation of method' or 'skilful means', while the sixth forms the 'accumulation of wisdom'.

Skilful Means (Skt *upaya*): The development of skilful compassion through the cultivation of the five 'method' perfections of generosity, discipline, patience, effort and concentration.

Sur (Tib. *gsur*): A burned substance or offering.

Three Jewels (Skt *triratna*): The Buddha or 'ultimate nature', the
dharma or teachings on the path to enlightenment, and the *sangha*
or perfect spiritual community.

Torma (Tib. *gtor-ma*): A ritual offering often modelled in the form
of a conical 'sacrificial cake' made from barley flour and butter.

FURTHER READING

Barks, Coleman & Moyne, John. *The Essential Rumi*, New York,
HarperCollins, 1995

Beer, Robert. *The Encyclopedia of Tibetan Symbols and Motifs*,
Boston, Shambhala Publications; Chicago and London, Serindia
Publications, 1999

Beer, Robert. *The Handbook of Tibetan Buddhist Symbols*, Boston,
Shambhala Publications; Chicago and London, Serindia
Publications, 2003

Dalai Lama. *Kindness, Clarity and Insight*, Ithaca, NY, Snow Lion
Publications, 1985

Dalai Lama. *The Meaning of Life from a Buddhist Perspective*, Boston,
Wisdom Publications, 1992

Khyentse, Dilgo. *The Heart Treasure of the Enlightened Ones*, Boston,
Shambhala Publications, 1992

Lama Lodo. *Bardo Teachings*, Ithaca, NY, Snow Lion Publications,
1982

Patrul Rinpoche. *The Words of My Perfect Teacher*, translated by
the Padmakara Translation Group, New York, HarperCollins, 1994

Trungpa, Chogyam. *Cutting Through Spiritual Materialism*, Boston,
Shambhala Publications, 1987

THE AUTHOR

Robert Beer is a distinguished artist and scholar of Buddhist and Hindu symbolism. He has studied and practised Tibetan *thangka* painting for over thirty years, and was one of the first Westerners to become actively involved in this art form. He is the author of *The Encyclopedia of Tibetan Symbols and Motifs* and *The Handbook of Tibetan Buddhist Symbols*, titles that have been highly acclaimed by Tibetan and Western scholars as definitive works. His paintings and drawings have appeared in more than 600 books on Buddhist themes.

ACKNOWLEDGEMENTS

I would like to thank Ian Jackson, Elaine Partington and the staff at Eddison Sadd Editions in London for being such a pleasure to work with, and to Liz Puttick for acting as my agent. My gratitude is also extended to my partner Gill Farrer-Halls for lovingly taking care of me during the writing of this text, to Phunsok Tshering of Nepal for overseeing the production of the ting-sha by the Tibetan craftsmen, to Karma Phunsok of Bhutan, whose father has been a lifelong practitioner of the *sur* ritual. Finally, I would like to thank the many different teachers and Tibetan lamas who have been a constant source of inspiration during my life, particularly the late Chagdud Rinpoche, whose abridged *sur* ritual I have included in this book, and to Linda Baer for facilitating this text.

EDDISON • SADD EDITIONS

Editorial Director	Ian Jackson	Art Director	Elaine Partington
Managing Editor	Tessa Monina	Art Editor	Pritty Ramjee
Copy-editor	Michele Turney	Mac Designer	Brazzle Atkins
Proofreader	Nikky Twyman	Production	Sarah Rooney and Nick Eddison